Discover India
State by State

OFF TO RAJASTHAN

SONIA MEHTA

PUFFIN BOOKS

An imprint of Penguin Random House

PUFFIN BOOKS

USA | Canada | UK | Ireland | Australia | New Zealand | India | South Africa | China | Singapore

Puffin Books is part of the Penguin Random House group of companies whose addresses can be found at global.penguinrandomhouse.com

Published by Penguin Random House India Pvt. Ltd
4th Floor, Capital Tower 1, MG Road,
Gurugram 122 002, Haryana, India

First published in Puffin Books by Penguin Random House India 2017

Text, design and illustrations copyright © Quadrum Solutions Pvt. Ltd 2017
Series copyright © Penguin Random House India 2017

Picture Credits
P 9: A herder with his camels (OlegD/Shutterstock.com); P 10: Great Indian Bustard (© Prajwalkm (Own work) [CC BY-SA 3.0 (http://creativecommons.org/licenses/by-sa/3.0)], via Wikimedia Commons); Camel (© Sandra Cohen-Rose and Colin Rose from Montreal, Canada (Camelot Uploaded by Ekabhishek) [CC BY-SA 2.0 (http://creativecommons.org/licenses/by-sa/2.0)], via Wikimedia Commons), Chinkara (© Pawar Pooja (Own work) [CC BY-SA 4.0 (http://creativecommons.org/licenses/by-sa/4.0), via Wikimedia Commons);P 11: Ranthambore (Dr Ajay Kumar Singh/Shutterstock.com); P 12: Bikaner (Salvador Aznar/Shutterstock.com); P 13: Jaipur (Radiokafka/Shutterstock.com); P 19: A Rajasthani man sitting on a camel (Nila Newsom/Shutterstock.com); P 24: Performances at the Pushkar Fair (Phuong D. Nguyen/Shutterstock.com); P 27: A performer with a sword in her mouth (MOROZ NATALIYA/Shutterstock.com); P 30: A Rajasthani haveli (gary yim/Shutterstock.com); P 35: Junagarh Fort (Vedaant Sethia/Shutterstock.com); P 36: Jantar Mantar, Jaipur (Don Mammoser/Shutterstock.com); P 41: Tourists on an elephant (MOROZ NATALIYA/Shutterstock.com); P 44: A traditional Rajasthani thali (© Meghana78 (Own work) [CC BY-SA 4.0 (http://creativecommons.org/licenses/by-sa/4.0)], via Wikimedia Commons); P 48: Rajasthani village huts (NataliaMilko/Shutterstock.com); P 49: A traditionally dressed Rajasthani man (Don Mammoser/Shutterstock.com), Man wearing flat pagri (Don Mammoser/Shutterstock.com); P 54: A room in a Rajasthan haveli (Radiokafka/Shutterstock.com)

The views and opinions expressed in this book are the author's own and the facts are as reported by her, which have been verified to the extent possible, and the publishers are not in any way liable for the same.

The information in this book is based on research from bona fide sites and published books and is true to the best of the author's knowledge at the time of going to print. The author is not responsible for any further changes or developments occurring post the publication of this book. This series is not a comprehensive representation of the states of India but is intended to give children a flavour of the lifestyles and cultures of different states. All illustrations are artistic representations only.

ISBN 9780143440802

Design and layout by Quadrum Solutions Pvt. Ltd
Printed at Repro India Limited

www.penguin.co.in

This is a legitimate digitally printed version of the book and therefore might not have certain extra finishing on the cover.

Hello Kids!

I'm so happy you are reading this book. India is an incredible country and there are lots of things about it that we never get to hear about.

I discovered India because my father was in the Indian army. He was posted to many places all over India—and we dutifully followed him. Can you imagine that by the time I was in the tenth standard, I had changed nine schools? Of course it was hard making new friends almost every year, but the good part was that I got to live in so many places. Right from Kerala, where I was born, to Kashmir, Jhansi, Shillong, Chandigarh, Goa . . . the list is long.

Every time I go to a new place, I feel amazed at how different each state is from the other—and yet, how similar. Did you know that we can see monuments from the Stone Age right here in India? Or that we have more than twenty official languages, and most Indians know three or four on an average? Or even that some of the world's most amazing scientific marvels were invented in India?

Oh, there are many, many, many fun and fantastic things about the states of India, which we simply must get to know.

So get your backpack ready, get set to meet some new friends, and join me on a fun trip as we DISCOVER INDIA, STATE BY STATE.

I hope you enjoy reading this book as much as I have enjoyed writing it. I would love to hear from you. So do write to me at sonia.mehta@quadrumltd.com.

Lots of love,
Sonia Aunty

Mishki and Pushka have come to visit Earth from their home planet, Zoomba. They have never seen such an amazing place. Zoomba doesn't have trees and mountains and rivers like Earth does. But the people look exactly the same. When they come to Earth, they meet a sweet old man whom they call Daadu Dolma. Daadu Dolma shows them all the wonderful places in India and tells Mishki and Pushka all about them.

Mishki and Pushka can't believe what they see. They have seen a lot of Earth, but they have never, ever seen a place like India.

They are off to explore India state by state :)

Mishki

Mishki is a curious little girl. She is always asking loads of questions. On her home planet, she is always getting into trouble for poking her nose into things that are not her business.

Pushka

Pushka is Mishki's brother. He loves adventure. He is always ready for a new challenge. Whether it's climbing a mountain, or diving into a cold, cold sea, he is up for it.

Daadu Dolma

Daadu Dolma is a wise old man who has lived on Earth longer than the mountains and the seas. No one knows quite how old he is, but he certainly has been around. He knows everything about everything.

Mishki and Pushka are about to visit one of India's most colourful states.

They have heard so much about it that they just can't wait.

'I've heard there is a beautiful desert in Rajasthan,' says Pushka. 'I want to ride a camel.'

'And I have heard there are beautiful buildings. I want to see them all,' says Mishki, clapping her hands.

'Well, you are both going to get your wish. Because Rajasthan has all of that and much, much more. So are you ready to leave?'

'Yes!' shout Mishki and Pushka together. They are

OFF TO RAJASTHAN!!!

Land ahoy!

Look, Pushka! The desert! Daadu, is the whole of Rajasthan a desert?

No, not at all. Rajasthan has many types of landforms. But the desert is the most famous because it is so vast and beautiful.

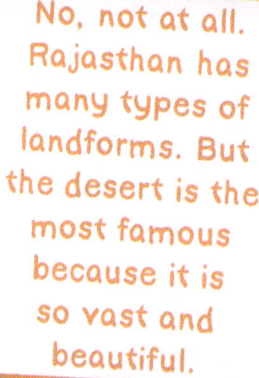

ON THE MAP

To see exactly where Rajasthan is on the map of India, go to http://www.mapsofindia.com/maps/india/india-political-map.htm

INDIA'S BIGGEST STATE

The lovely state of Rajasthan is India's largest state, area wise. It is in the north-west of India and shares a long, long border with Pakistan. But it has many other neighbours too. Punjab, Uttar Pradesh, Haryana, Madhya Pradesh and Gujarat are all right next door!

SANDY AND ROCKY

Rajasthan has rocky terrain and rolling sand dunes. But it also has wetlands, river-drained plains, plateaus, ravines and wooded areas. Basically, Rajasthan has four clear regions:

1 The Aravalli or hilly region

2 The fertile plains that include Mewar

3 Water bodies that include the state's few rivers and lakes

4 The magnificent Thar Desert and other dry shrub lands

With plateaus that include the Vindhya and Malwa Plateaus

OLD, OLD MOUNTAINS

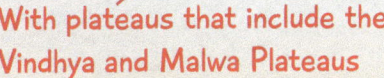

Rajasthan has one of India's oldest mountain ranges, the Aravalli Range. The highest point of this range is Mount Abu—a very famous place for tourists and pilgrims because of its temples. Despite the mountains, Rajasthan has very little forest area. This is because the soil here is generally dry and salty, making it hard for plants to grow.

EXTREME WEATHER

Oh, yes! Rajasthan's weather is extreme, all right. Winters are freezing, but summers are so hot, you can barely stand outdoors.

JUST DESERT!

The Thar Desert, which makes up most of Rajasthan, is a magnificent desert with miles and miles of sand. Most of it is in Rajasthan, but a part of it also goes into Pakistan. The sand has been deposited by wind over more than a million years. You will see it in wavy dunes, some high and some low. These dunes are separated from each other by sandy plains and low hills called *bhakars*.

The dunes keep changing shape with the wind. They form patterns that locals call *dhoras*.

DINOSAURS? REALLY?

Just imagine! Archaeologists believe that long, long ago, dinosaurs must have roamed this region, which was once lush and green. Now, of course, it is dry, with hardly any rainfall. There's just one brave river called Luni, which struggles through the desert, giving the residents here some relief.

SALT LAKES

There are lakes in the desert too, though the water is salty. These are called *playas* or *dhands*. So naturally, water here is very scarce.

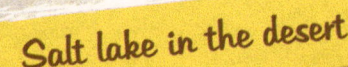
Salt lake in the desert

A herder with his camels

SO HARD TO LIVE

Living in the desert is tough—for people, animals and plants too! Many people who reside here are nomadic. They live in groups and camps, often moving from place to place on camels to escape the harsh weather. There are a few tough plants and shrub-like trees that struggle to survive. Some animals, like blackbucks and gazelles, and birds, like sandgrouses, wild ducks and geese, can be seen here.

Blackbucks

Bar-headed geese

Check out the two black bars on the head of the geese

The desert is also home to the great Indian bustard, an endangered species.

WHAT'S ODD?

In each of the rows below, one word doesn't belong. Which one is it?

| SAND | DUNE | DESERT | OCEAN |

| PLAINS | PLATEAUS | SKYSCRAPERS | WETLANDS |

| ARAVALLI | VINDHYA | LUNI | MALWA |

RIVER FACTS

The Aravalli range is like the watershed of Rajasthan. Most of its rivers start in the folds of this range. The Chambal River is the only river that is full all year. The other main rivers are the Luni, the Banas and the Banganga, which try their best to keep this dry state from being thirsty.

Chambal River

Pearl Millet (Bajra)

CROP SHOP

Rajasthan is a dry state, yet farmers do a good job growing crops here. Many types of crops are grown—though not in huge quantities. Wheat and barley grow in the areas that are fertile. Corn and millet manage to grow even in comparatively dry regions. Rice grows in areas that have plenty of irrigation, as rice needs lots of water.

FUN FACTS

State tree
Khejri

State flower
Rohida

State Animal
Chinkara

State Animal
Camel

State bird
The Indian bustard

The roaring king of Ranthambhore

RANTHAMBHORE TIGER RESERVE

WILD WONDERS

Even though Rajasthan does not have a lot of forest area, it is still rich in wildlife. The famous Ranthambore Wildlife Sanctuary is best known for the magnificent tiger. There are lots of other wild animals too, like langurs, jungle cats, civets, foxes, porcupines and five-striped palm squirrels. Great care is taken to protect and preserve these creatures, many of which (like the tiger) are endangered.

PORCUPINE TWINS

Look! Mishki and Pushka have spotted some porcupines. Can you tell which two porcupines are exactly alike?

A

B

C

D

CITY CITY BANG BANG

Bikaner

THE DESERT TRIANGLE

There are three big cities in Rajasthan that sort of form a triangle. These cities are:

Bikaner, Jaisalmer and Jodhpur.

The Blue City: Jodhpur is called the Blue City because its houses are painted blue. Its forts and palaces are visited by people from across the world.

Medieval Charm: Bikaner is a desert city that is dotted with sand dunes. It's called Camel Country due to the number of camel carts that carry people and goods on the city's busy streets.

The Golden City: Jaisalmer is called the Golden City because the sand dunes here cast a golden light in the evening sun. This city is full of palaces and forts and has a rich history.

Jodhpur

Jaisalmer

THE PINK CITY

Jaipur, the capital of Rajasthan, is also called the Pink City because many of its buildings were painted a unique shade of pink by Maharaja Ram Singh. It is full of historic buildings.

Pink was considered the colour of hospitality. So when Queen Victoria of England was to visit the city, Maharaja Ram Singh painted the whole city pink!

THE HOLY CITY

The city of Ajmer is holy for people of all religions. This is mainly because of the shrine of a Muslim saint, whom people lovingly call Khwaja. He believed in peace and brotherhood. People of all religions visit this shrine to pray.

THE CITY OF LAKES

The beautiful city of Udaipur sits pretty on Lake Pichola. It's named after Maharana Udai Singh II. It is surrounded by the Aravalli range and is dotted with exquisite palaces.

Long, long ago

Daadu, everywhere I look there are palaces and forts. Why is that?

That's because Rajasthan has had a lot of kings, many wars and a rich history we are going to learn all about.

LAND OF THE RAJPUTS

We always think of the Rajputs as courageous warriors. Rajasthan's history is full of tales of their bravery. Many Rajput dynasties ruled over Rajputana. A dynasty called the Gurjara-Pratiharas fought the Arabs who tried to invade from the Sindh area—which is now in Pakistan. This dynasty managed to carve their empire through their part of North India. But finally, after some weak rulers, this dynasty disintegrated.

Rajasthan literally translates to 'land of the kings'—'raja' (king) and 'sthan' (land).

MANY RULERS, MANY CLANS

Many different Rajput clans began to fight for supremacy. You must have heard several of these names. Small clans like the Chauhans, Bhattis, Rathors and Kachwahas all set up their own kingdoms within Rajputana. Oh, they would fight each other from time to time, but they also coexisted for a long time.

HIDDEN WORDS

How many words can you make from the word RAJPUTANA?
Mishki has made ten.

R A J P U T A N A

A NEW ERA

A king called Muhammad of Ghor had set his sights on Rajasthan. He fought a fierce battle with Prithviraj III and defeated him. For 400 years the Rajput kings had held off invaders. But now they were too weak to withstand the onslaughts.

Babur

Rana Sanga

THE BEGINNING OF THE END OF THE RAJPUTS

A king called Rana Sanga from Mewar in Rajasthan fought a fierce battle against the Mughal ruler Babur. He was defeated, and after this, the Rajput kings slowly began to lose their strength. King after king gave in to the Mughals.

THE RULE OF THE MUGHALS

The Mughal Empire began to spread across India. Almost all of Rajasthan was under the Mughals. Akbar the Great came into power. He defeated the few strongholds the Rajputs still had—like Ranthambore and Chittaurgarh—and destroyed them completely.

SMART MOVE

Akbar was smart. He defeated the Rajput kings but remained friends with them. He married a Rajput princess and planned similar marriages for his sons. Thanks to this clever move, the Rajput kings gave in to Mughal rule without resistance. They were part of the family now. Many Rajput kings even fought as a part of the Mughal army.

There are stories of great valour and bravery told about some famous Rajput kings. Rana Uday Singh, his son Pratap Singh, Prithviraj Chauhan, Bappa Rawal and Rana Kumbha are some brave Rajput kings.

Akbar married Rajput princess Jodha

WORD GRID

Look at all the names of kings and dynasties hidden in this grid. Can you find them all? Babur, Akbar, Mughals, Rana Sanga, Rathor, Pratap Singh, Bhattis

B	A	B	U	R	A	H	S	N	A	S
P	R	A	T	A	P	S	I	N	G	H
S	A	S	D	M	U	G	H	A	L	S
R	A	T	H	O	R	F	F	G	H	M
X	V	B	N	M	G	T	P	T	A	Y
A	K	B	A	R	Q	W	E	R	T	H
R	R	A	N	A	S	A	N	G	A	N
D	Q	S	B	H	A	T	T	I	S	N

END OF THE MUGHALS

After Akbar, his descendants ruled for many years. His grandson Aurangzeb was the last powerful Mughal ruler. Aurangzeb did a lot of things that angered the Rajputs. After him, his sons and grandsons led lavish lives and didn't do much for the empire. The Mughals were defeated soon after.

THE BRITISH ARE ON THE SCENE

The British had their eyes on India. They wanted to make it a British colony—which means they wanted to rule in their own way. They started by trading with India. But soon, they defeated the Mughals and Marathas and took control of the whole country. India became a British colony. But Indians wanted the British to leave them alone and let them be independent.

FIGHT FOR INDEPENDENCE

Now the whole of India was united against a common enemy—the British. They had made many laws that were unfair to Indians. Ajmer, in Rajasthan, was a centre of activity in the independence struggle against the British. India finally became independent in 1947.

TODAY'S RAJASTHAN IS BORN

There were many kings in Rajasthan who had land but no power. After the British left, the power was now in the hands of the Indian government. It was decided that the princely states would be brought together under one state—Rajasthan. For many years after independence, several kings still had privileges. In 1970, even those were stopped and the kings became ordinary citizens.

Spot the Difference

Pushka has just seen two pictures of decorated elephants.

Find ten differences in the two pictures given here.

Talk time

Wow! The history of this state is so interesting. But what language do all these people speak, Daadu? Has it changed over the years?

Yes, of course it has. Apart from Hindi, Rajasthan has its own languages and dialects. In fact, these were born from the languages spoken by the Indo-Aryan people thousands and thousands of years ago.

NEW LANGUAGES ARE BORN

Many centuries ago, poets and singers sang praises of their masters in a language called Dingal. From this language were born other dialects that people in Rajasthan speak today.

Maheshwari

Marwari

Jaipuri or Dhundhari

Malvi

Mewati

COMMON MARWARI

Hello = Khamma Gani or Khammaosa

Goodbye = Khamma Gani

Yes = Ha/Hamme

No = Na/koni

How much money? = Kitto peso?

What is your name? = Tharo naam kay hai?

I don't understand = Manney samajh kon padhey

What? = Kay?

Go = Jawo

MATCH THE WORDS

Pushka remembers the new words she's heard. Do you? Match the English words to their Rajasthani meanings.

English	Rajasthani
What?	Khamma Gani
How much money?	Hamme
Go	Kay?
Goodbye	Kitto peso?
Yes	Tharo naam kay hai?
What is your name?	Jawo

A peep into their life

Oh, Daadu! I love the way people look and dress and talk here. They are so colourful. Are they like this all over Rajasthan?

Oh no! Rajasthan has different regions. People living in the desert are quite different from people in cities.

PATCHWORK OF PEOPLE

There are many communities in Rajasthan. The tribal people who roam the desert; the farming community; the Rajput descendants; the trading community—all these people share many festivals and traditions, but they have their own unique ones too! Hindus are the majority, while Muslims the second largest. Jainism also has a strong presence in Rajasthan.

WRITE STYLES

Rajasthan's literature is rich and ancient. A lot of it was never written but passed down orally through generations. An epic poem called Prithviraj Raso, written by a man called Chand Bardai, is more than 800 years old. Wow!

STORIES OF THE PAST

People say that among the oldest literature of Rajasthan are the stories written by a writer named Suryamal Misrama. He wrote stories about the lives of Rajput kings and princes and about war heroes of that time. We know so much about life in those days from these tales and poems.

SONGS OF PROTEST

During the independence struggle, poets wrote songs to inspire people. Poets like Hiralala Sastri, Manikyalala Varma and Jayanarayana Vyasa urged people to keep the fight going.

RHYME TIME

Mishki is also going to write a song about kings. She needs to find five words that rhyme with KING. Can you help her?

K I N G

FANTASTIC FESTIVALS AND FAIRS

Rajasthan is called a colourful state with good reason. It has loads and loads of festivals and fairs that are great fun and so different from other parts of India.

PUSHKAR FAIR

Legend goes that millions of years ago, on a full moon night, Lord Vishnu created Pushkar Lake. The Pushkar Mela (or fair) is a grand five-day celebration of this magical event. For over a hundred years, people have been collecting around this lake on a particular full moon night some time during October or November. Millions of tourists and pilgrims come to this fair. Besides taking a dip in Pushkar Lake, they enjoy camel races, colourful dances and amazing food.

The length of a man's moustache is a sign of his strength and importance. Men actually have moustache contests during the Pushkar Mela.

GANGAUR

Gana and Gauri

During this festival, women pray for a happy married life. Gangaur stands for Gana (Lord Shiva) and Gauri (his wife). Unmarried girls fast for a good husband. Each of them carries an idol of Gauri and, singing songs, they immerse these idols in water. This is their farewell to Gauri as she goes to her husband's home. Sweets called ghevar and ghughari are cooked during this time.

URS

This festival honours the Muslim saint Khwaja Moinuddin Chisti. His tomb in Ajmer is the centre of this festival. For six days, his followers, who are from many different religions, pray to him. They place a *chadar* (or holy cloth) on the tomb. Rice is cooked in giant pots. All night long, devotees sing qawwali songs, which are a special type of spiritual music.

CROSSWORD TIME

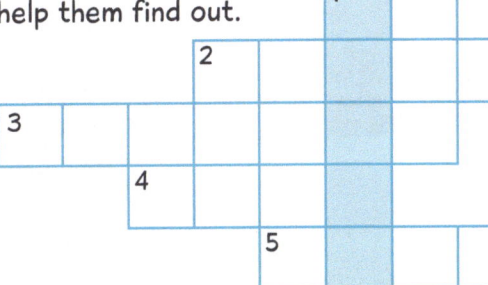

Mishki and Pushka want to find out the name hidden in the blue squares. Solve the clues and help them find out.

1. A tasty sweet made during a popular festival.

2. The holy cloth people place on the tomb of Khwaja Moinuddin Chisti.

3. A popular festival during which women fast.

4. The event at Pushkar where camel races are held.

5. The name of the god who people say has created Pushkar Lake.

THE DANCE OF PUPPETS

The Kathputhli, or the puppet dance, is supposed to be more than a thousand years old. It began in a community called Bhattis. Puppeteers would perform this to entertain kings and queens. They would create colourful wooden puppets and show off their skills by making the puppets do swordplay, horse riding, juggling and acrobatics.

GHOOM GHOOM GHOOMAR

The Ghoomar is one of Rajasthan's most famous dances. Women dance in a circle, twirling away. Their colourful ghaghras billow around them. Although people say it originated in the Bhil tribe, now everyone does this dance. As the beat and tempo of the music increase, the dancers start spinning faster and faster.

HORSING AROUND

Once, bandits roamed in a place called Shekhawati. When traders passed by with their wares, these robbers would attack them. The Kachi Ghodi dance depicts a fight between the traders and bandits. Men perform this dance on dummy horses. Songs narrating stories of those bygone days are performed.

A FIRE DANCE

This amazing dance describes the lifestyle of a tribe called Jasnathis. It was believed that these people had magical powers. On a large ground, burning coal and charcoal is spread. Men jump and dance to drum beats while on top of this mixture. They also do stunts with fire rods and blow flames from their mouths.

THE DRUM DANCE

Usually men do this dance. They beat enormous drums tied around their necks. A dancer, with huge cymbals, accompanies them. He also juggles swords as he dances. Often a woman joins the dance, holding a sword in her mouth!

It sure needs a lot of skill to do this dance.

Bricks and Stones

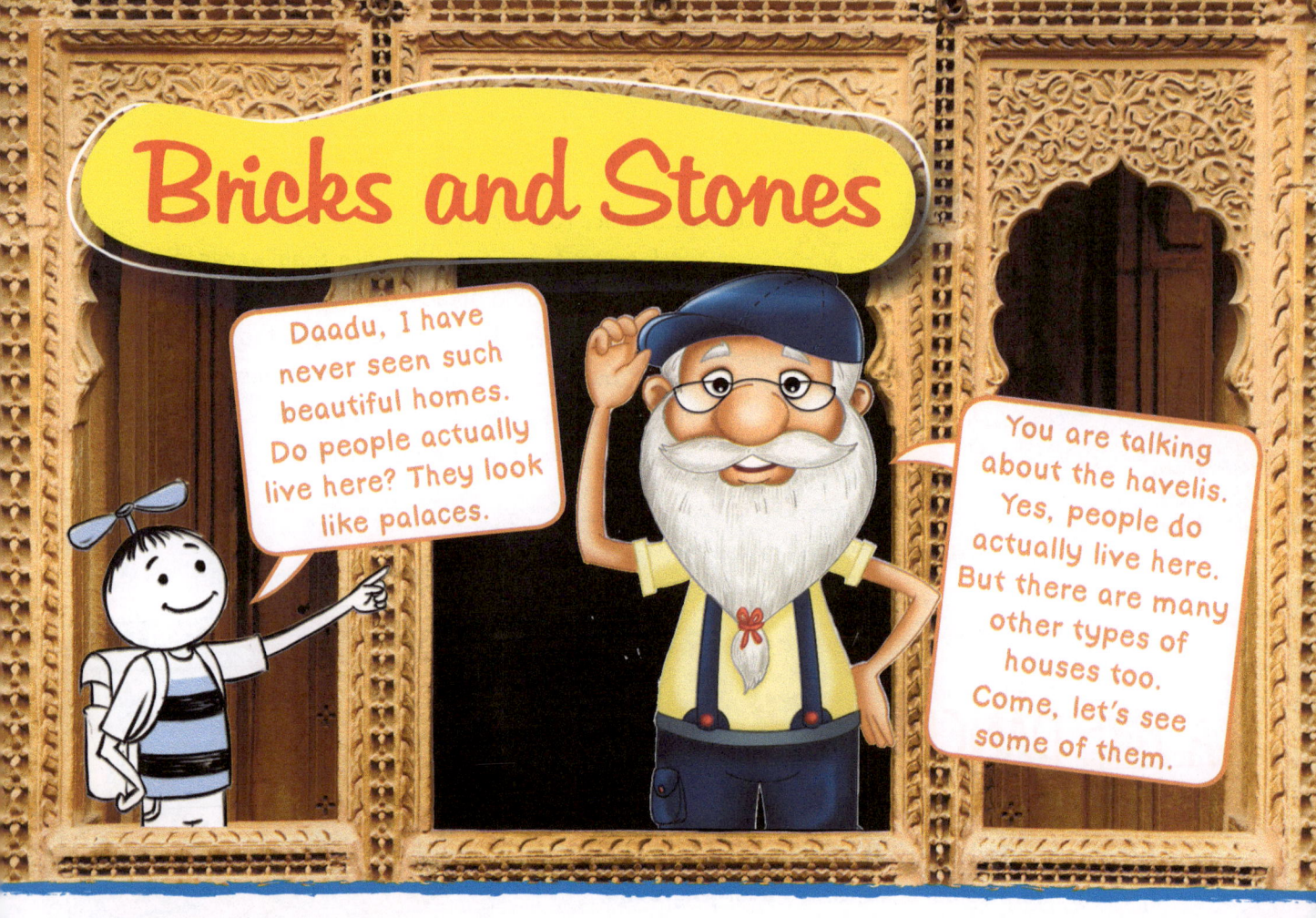

Daadu, I have never seen such beautiful homes. Do people actually live here? They look like palaces.

You are talking about the havelis. Yes, people do actually live here. But there are many other types of houses too. Come, let's see some of them.

HUTS APLENTY

As such a large part of Rajasthan is desert, it is one of India's least populated states. In rural places, farmers build mud huts with roofs of straw. These have just one door and few or no windows. The mud floors are coated with cow dung. The slightly wealthier farmers have proper houses with tiles. But their front doors are large enough for a bullock cart to pass through. Gosh!

It sounds yucky but cow dung is one of the most hygienic and comfortable floor coverings.

TOWN PLANNING

We've seen that so much of Rajasthan is dry and desert like. From the beginning, people had to build homes that would protect them from the harsh sun in summer, and keep them cosy during winter. That is why in Rajasthan towns, you will see buildings huddled together, so that they give each other shade and also give shade to people walking on the streets.

DUST FREE

Because of the desert, there are a lot of dust storms in several parts of Rajasthan. Many houses have solid walls with very small windows or openings. Even the streets are built in an east-west direction to block dust from these storms.

ECO-FRIENDLY

Many walls in traditional Rajasthani homes are made from natural stones that help keep the inside cool. On the outside, however, you will see deeply carved patterns. This is because a flat surface heats up more than a carved surface. These are all clever little tricks that the builders of yore used to fight the harsh elements.

Carved patterns

Print Patterns

Look at this pattern that Mishki saw on a wall of one of the houses. Can you draw and colour it in exactly the same way?

HAVELI HO!

The first havelis were built by rich Marwari people for their large joint families. There would be grandparents, parents, aunts, uncles, nieces, nephews and children all living together in family homes. The different regions of Rajasthan had their own types of havelis.

'Haveli' comes from the Persian word 'howli'—meaning an enclosed area.

TYPES AND TYPES OF HAVELIS

There are many kinds of havelis. Some are magnificent, almost like palaces, with many courtyards and hundreds of rooms, while some are modest, with just about twenty rooms and a single courtyard. But what they all have in common are intricate carvings on doors, frescoes showing wars or religious scenes and wonderful stained-glass windows. Let's see some features that all havelis have.

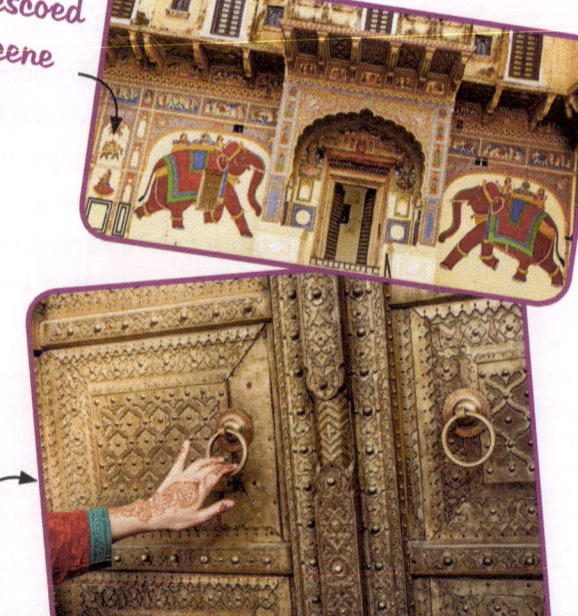

Frescoed scene

Carved doors

COURTYARDS

All havelis have at least one courtyard. Some have more. One courtyard could be demarcated as an open-air kitchen. Another would be used only by the menfolk, and yet another by women.

JHAROKHA: THE BALCONY

Many havelis have a hanging balcony called a jharokha. One of the main uses of this was for women to peep out from, in such a way that they could see but not be seen.

JOHAD: THE WATER TANK

All havelis had their own water tank in which they would collect the scarce rain water. It was used for drinking and cooking all through the year.

CHATTRI: THE PORCH

Chattris are dome-shaped porches. Sometimes they were built at the entrance of a grand haveli; other times as stand-alone structures. The bigger the chhattri, the more important and wealthy the owner.

FAMOUS HAVELIS

There are many famous havelis in which families no longer live. They are now tourist attractions for visitors to see how people lived in the grand old days. The Patwon ki Haveli is famous. It is a cluster of five havelis that were built by a banker named Guman Chand Patwa.

Patwon ki Haveli

Standing strong

Daadu, look! Such beautiful palaces. I want to explore them.

No, first I want to climb those amazing forts.

We can do both. Because Rajasthan is full of palaces and forts. And much more! We will see it all.

The walls of the fort are almost six metres thick—as much as the length of a room.

MEHRANGARH FORT

Mehrangarh Fort in Jodhpur is one of India's largest forts. There are palaces inside this fort. Each palace used to have a different function. There is the Moti Mahal (Palace of Pearls) in which the royal throne of Jodhpur is. The Phool Mahal (Palace of Flowers) is full of paintings of musical moods. The Jhanki Mahal (Peeping Palace) is where all the queens and royal women watched the comings and goings from.

CHITTORGARH

This incredible fort sure has seen a lot of action. Wars, murders, sieges and a whole lot of excitement. The fort is named after the Rajput king Chitrangada Mori. It has seven massive entrances. There are even temples, reservoirs and palaces inside this enormous fort.

RANI PADMAVATI OF CHITTORGARH

When Sultan Alauddin Khilji heard of Rani Padmavati's beauty, he wanted to see her. He caught a glimpse of her reflection in a water tank. He fell so in love that he fought a war for her. But he could not win her, because she sacrificed her life in order to not be wedded to him.

JAISALMER FORT

This is India's only 'living' fort. This means people actually still live inside it. It is over 800 years old. It looks golden because it is made entirely of yellow sandstone. It is right in the middle of the magnificent Thar Desert. This amazing fort has ninety-nine turrets. There are Jain temples inside that are more than 700 years old. Today, there are homes, shops and restaurants all inside this amazing fort.

Turrets

AMER FORT

This is a really old fort, built at a time when Amer was the state capital. It is a mix of both Rajput and Mughal architecture. Its strong walls have withstood many bloody battles between the Rajputs and Mughals. Now, of course, visitors can go and admire its palaces, courtyards and lakes, and just try to imagine how life must have been hundreds of years ago.

Did you know? The Amer fort has been declared a World Heritage Site.

THAT'S SCARY!

THE HAUNTED FORT

Now here's an exciting story. The Bhangarh Fort was built by Man Singh I. People believe this fort is haunted and no one is allowed to be inside it after dark. Scary! The legend is that there was an evil wizard who fell in love with a beautiful princess called Ratnavati. He gave her a potion that would make her fall in love with him too. But she threw it on a boulder, which rolled down a hill and crushed the wizard. Before he died, he cursed her and the entire kingdom. People believe that the ghosts of Ratnavati and the wizard roam the fort at night.

JUNAGARH FORT

This lovely fort in Bikaner was built and added to for over 400 years. It is one of the few forts that is not built on the top of a hill or mountain. There are beautiful temples, palaces and pavilions inside the fort. Every time a new king came to live here, he would build new rooms and palaces. You can imagine how wars were fought when you see iron spikes poking out of the gates, to keep charging elephants out. Ouch!

Maharaja's resting room with arches in gold-patterns

Amazing Maze

Mishki and Pushka are lost in this royal lake. Help them find their way out.

THE PALACE OF WINDS

The Hawa Mahal in Jaipur is really famous. Do you know why? Not just because it is beautiful but also because it has been built so cleverly—its many, many windows catch the breeze in just the right way, making the palace cool even in a hot and dry place like Jaipur. The other exciting thing about it is that it has almost a thousand windows with intricate patterns. These were created so that the royal ladies could look out at the streets without being seen.

JANTAR MANTAR

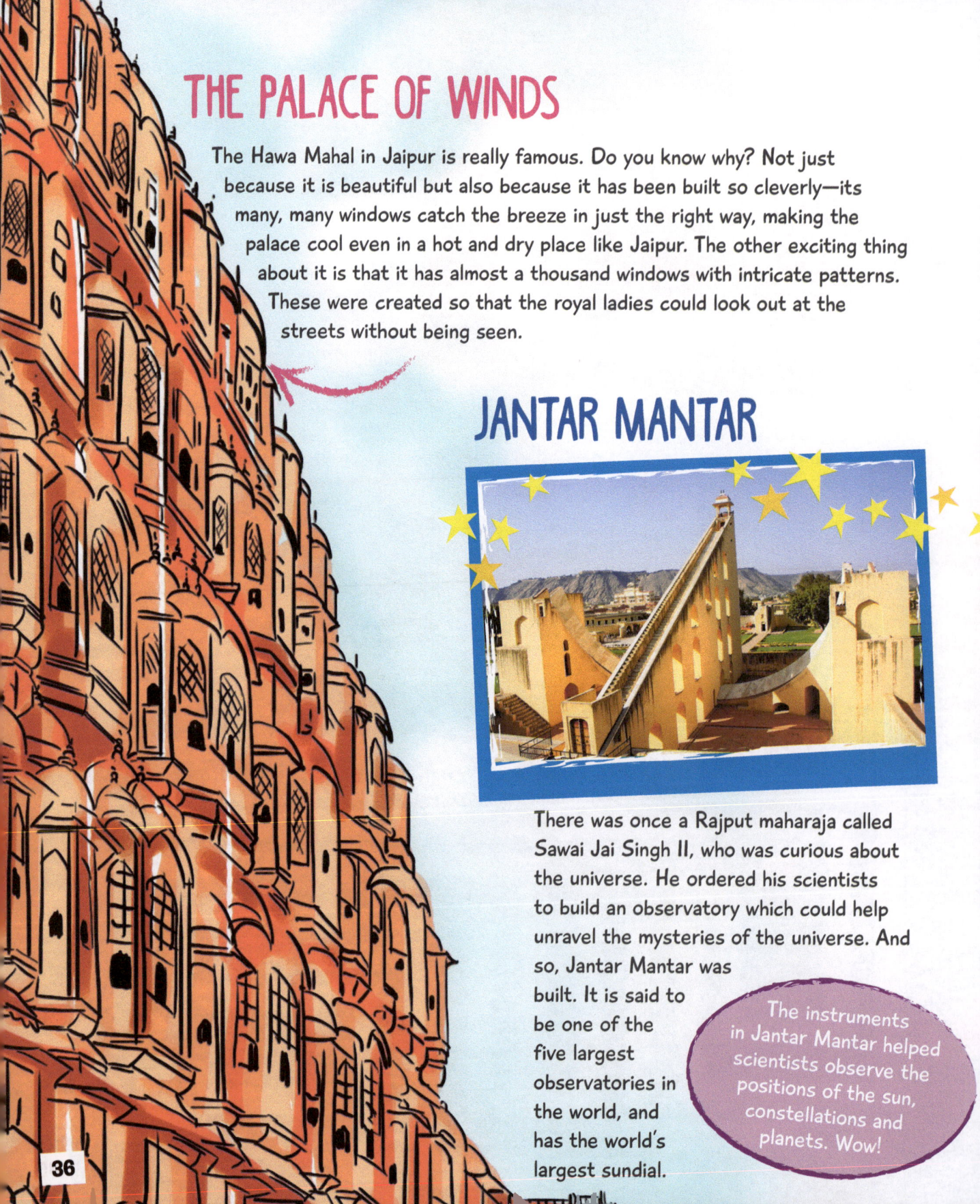

There was once a Rajput maharaja called Sawai Jai Singh II, who was curious about the universe. He ordered his scientists to build an observatory which could help unravel the mysteries of the universe. And so, Jantar Mantar was built. It is said to be one of the five largest observatories in the world, and has the world's largest sundial.

The instruments in Jantar Mantar helped scientists observe the positions of the sun, constellations and planets. Wow!

THE WATER PALACE

The Jal Mahal perches prettily on the Man Sagar Lake in Jaipur. To reach the palace, maharajas had to take a wooden boat. And guess what? The same boats have been recreated so that you can be rowed across the lake just like royalty. How cool! It's not just that the palace is on a lake—it's also surrounded by hills. There are lovely migratory birds around here too, which add to the beauty of the palace.

EXACTLY!!

Which two images of the sundial are exactly the same? Can you find out?

A

B

C

D

THE WONDER OF RANAKPUR

There is a magnificent Jain temple in Ranakpur, built by a Jain businessman called Seth Dharna Sah with the help of the ruler of Mewar—Rana Kumbha. It has over 1400 pillars. Each pillar has carvings and no two are alike. There are many mini-temples inside. The temple is made of marble, and it changes colour every hour because of the changing sunlight.

Did you know? They say it took nearly sixty-five years to build this temple. Wow!

ON TOP OF MOUNT ABU

People say that the Dilwara Temples at Mount Abu are among the finest Jain temples in the world. Know why? Some believe that the craftsmanship is even better than that of the Taj Mahal. They're over 800 years old. Elephants were used to transport enormous blocks of marble to the top of the mountains.

A TEMPLE WITH A LEGEND

One day, Lord Brahma saw that an evil demon was harassing people. Lord Brahma was so powerful that he defeated the demon using just a lotus flower as a weapon. The petals of the lotus fell to earth. And that is where Pushkar Lake appeared. Brahma then decided to pray by the lake and created a temple where he stood. This is the famous Brahma Temple at Pushkar.

EKLINGJI TEMPLE

This temple near Udaipur is dedicated to Lord Shiva. It is different from most other temples because the main idol of Lord Shiva is made of black marble. It has lovely silver doors that depict Lord Ganesha and Lord Kartikeya guarding their father, Lord Shiva. Thousands of people come to pray at this temple.

WHAT'S ODD?

In each row, there is one word that is odd. Can you find out which one it is?

RANAKPUR	HAWA MAHAL	EKLINGJI	DILWARA
GANESHA	KARTIKEYA	SHIVA	AKBAR
UDAIPUR	MOUNT ABU	PUSHKAR	MUMBAI

Daadu, people built so many beautiful buildings here. But what do they do for a living now?

Rajasthan is a very unique state, Pushka. The people are very resourceful and innovative. Come, I'll tell you all about what they do.

BUSINESS IN THEIR BLOOD

As we've seen, a large part of Rajasthan is a dry desert. This is why, centuries ago, people living here began to look for other means to earn a living. They became traders, buying and selling things. Many years later, this ability to do business remains a talent. A lot of people from this energetic state have built huge businesses.

Businessmen used to conduct their work while on a gadda (mattress).

TOURIST PARADISE

With so many magnificent monuments, forts and palaces, there are bound to be tourists. Most foreign tourists make sure they stop in Rajasthan to see how royal India lived. In fact, many palaces and forts have even been turned into hotels. So you have lots of people working in this business—in hotels, airlines or as tour guides.

What fun it must be to show people around!

HOW PRECIOUS!

Rajasthan produces a good amount of precious stones—mainly emeralds and garnets. Perhaps that is why jewellery making is a big business. And, of course, the state has had so many royal families over the centuries, all of whom loved jewellery. So there are many people who work in the jewellery business too!

Emerald

Precious Stone Sudoku

Complete this precious stone sudoku. Make sure that each row and column has one of each precious stone.

AMAZING ARTISANS

Rajasthan has a long, long tradition of people working as craftsmen. From the Banjara and Bhil tribes to puppet and toy makers, Rajasthani crafts are known the world over.

CRAFTING FABRIC PATTERNS

The craftsmen of Rajasthan are famous for the wonderful designs they create on fabric. Block-printers, tie-dye craftsmen, striped leheriya-print artists. . .and oh! mirror-work specialists! They are all world famous.

Block-printing

PERFECT PAINTERS

For centuries, the artists of Rajasthan have been painting beautiful paintings—on walls, on cloth and as miniatures. They have become masters at making the most brilliant colours using crushed precious stones, vegetable dyes and even shells. Pichwai paintings are intricate depictions of Lord Krishna.

Wooden heads

Move with strings

PUPPET ON A STRING

The puppet makers of Rajasthan are truly talented. Many families have been puppet makers for generations. The handmade puppets are designed to be able to move fluidly on a string. With gaily painted wooden heads, the bodies are made with fabric and stuffed with cotton.

Do It Yourself
Sock Puppet

Mishki has made a sock puppet. You can make one too! Here's how.

1. Take an old sock and stick two buttons on it for eyes.

Simple, isn't it?

2. Cut some wool and stick in on for hair.

3. Put your hand into the sock to make your puppet move.

FOOD WITH A DIFFERENCE

Do you know why Rajasthani food is known to be different? Because so much of the state is a desert, leafy vegetables and fruit are not easy to come by. But that doesn't stop the people here in the least. They've come up with a style of cooking that uses the dry ingredients available to them, making the most amazing food out of lentils, pulses and even the bark of certain trees. Not just that—a lot of the food can last for days without having to be frozen or even reheated.

Let's see some of these dishes.

GATTE KI SABZI

This is a clever dish that is made entirely without any vegetables. Gram flour balls are steamed and popped into a yummy gravy made with buttermilk and spices. Eat this with rotis and you'll feel full for a nice, long while.

DAL BATI-CHURMA

This dish is made of bati (wheat dumplings) which are crushed and eaten with a yummy dal. To round off the taste, there is a sweet powder made of jaggery and wheat. It's all topped off with a dollop of ghee. Eat this amazing dish when you have a couple of hours to snooze after.

Dal

Bati

Churma

LAAL MAAS

This literally means red meat. In olden times, Rajput kings and princes would go on shikar. They would hunt deer and wild boar. The royal cooks would then make a meat curry that was red-hot and very rich. This is laal maas.

The Rajputs of Rajasthan simply adore this tasty dish.

AAM KI LAUNJI

This is a sweet and sour pickle made of raw mangoes. It's thick like a gravy and the mango pieces just explode in your mouth. People from Rajasthan love eating this along with their meals.

Ker   Sangri

KER SANGRI

Now here's a dish with a story. There was a great famine across India. A shrub with dull green berries, called ker, grew in the desert. A tree called khejari yielded dry beans. With nothing else to eat, the natives decided to make this work. They put these two ingredients together and what they got was a dish that is now a must during the most lavish Rajasthani weddings.

GHEVAR

This super rich sweet dish is made during festivals like Teej and Diwali. It is a disc shaped cake made with flour and soaked in sugar syrup. Sounds yummy (and heavy too).

GUJIYA

This half-moon shaped dessert can make your senses soar. This is a dumpling, cut and shaped like a semicircle. It is stuffed with sweetened and reduced milk, as well as dry fruits. It's then fried. It comes to your plate glistening golden and delicious. Don't eat too many at one go. This is super rich and super heavy!

Mixed-Up Words

Can you find the Rajasthani dishes in these mixed-up words?

A	Y	I	J	U	G
R	A	V	E	H	G
I	J	N	U	A	L
I	T	A	B		

Psst!! Try going backwards.

47

What to wear?

Daadu, look at those lovely skirts with mirror-work. I want to wear one.

We will get you one. You will see that many people in Rajasthan wear very colourful clothes.

BRIGHT COLOURS

Maybe because the landscape is so brown, people from Rajasthan simply love colour.

Women, especially in tribal areas, wear a long skirt that flares out wide like an umbrella when they swirl. This is called a ghaghra. It is usually a little short, so that they can show off their beautiful anklets.

Anklet

They wear this skirt with a long blouse that has brilliant mirror-work and colourful embroidery.

Mirror Work

The ensemble is completed with an *odhani*—a long cloth that they drape over their shoulders. It's normally in a traditional print, like leheriya. They also use this to cover their heads.

TURBAN TREND

Men wear very elaborate turbans called pagris. They say the colour and the style in which it is tied tells people the caste and region that the wearer belongs to. In Udaipur, men wear a flat pagri. In Jodhpur, the pagri is worn in curved bands. For the rest of their clothing, men wear a dhoti, or pyjamas, and a waistband. During festivals, they add on a colourful waistcoat called an *angarakha*.

Flat pagri

Pagri with curved bands

FOOTSIE

Both men and women wear shoes that are made of camel, sheep or goat skin. These are called *mojris*. Sometimes the mojris are dressed up with embroidery or mirror-work.

Shoes made of camel, sheep or goat skin

TURBAN TRICK

Pushka wants to try on a turban. Can you find the two turbans that are exactly alike?

A   B   C   D

Autograph, please?

I have my autograph book all ready, Daadu. Who are we going to meet?

We are going to know more about famous people from this wonderful state. Some are not alive any more, but they are still very famous.

GOVINDRAM SEKSARIA

He was called the 'Cotton King of India'. He was one of the most successful businessmen in India before Independence. He built a huge business empire dealing in cotton.

VIJAYDAN DETHA

He was known as the Shakespeare of Rajasthan. He wrote short stories based on folk tales. He was nominated for the Nobel Prize, and won many awards, including the Padma Shri.

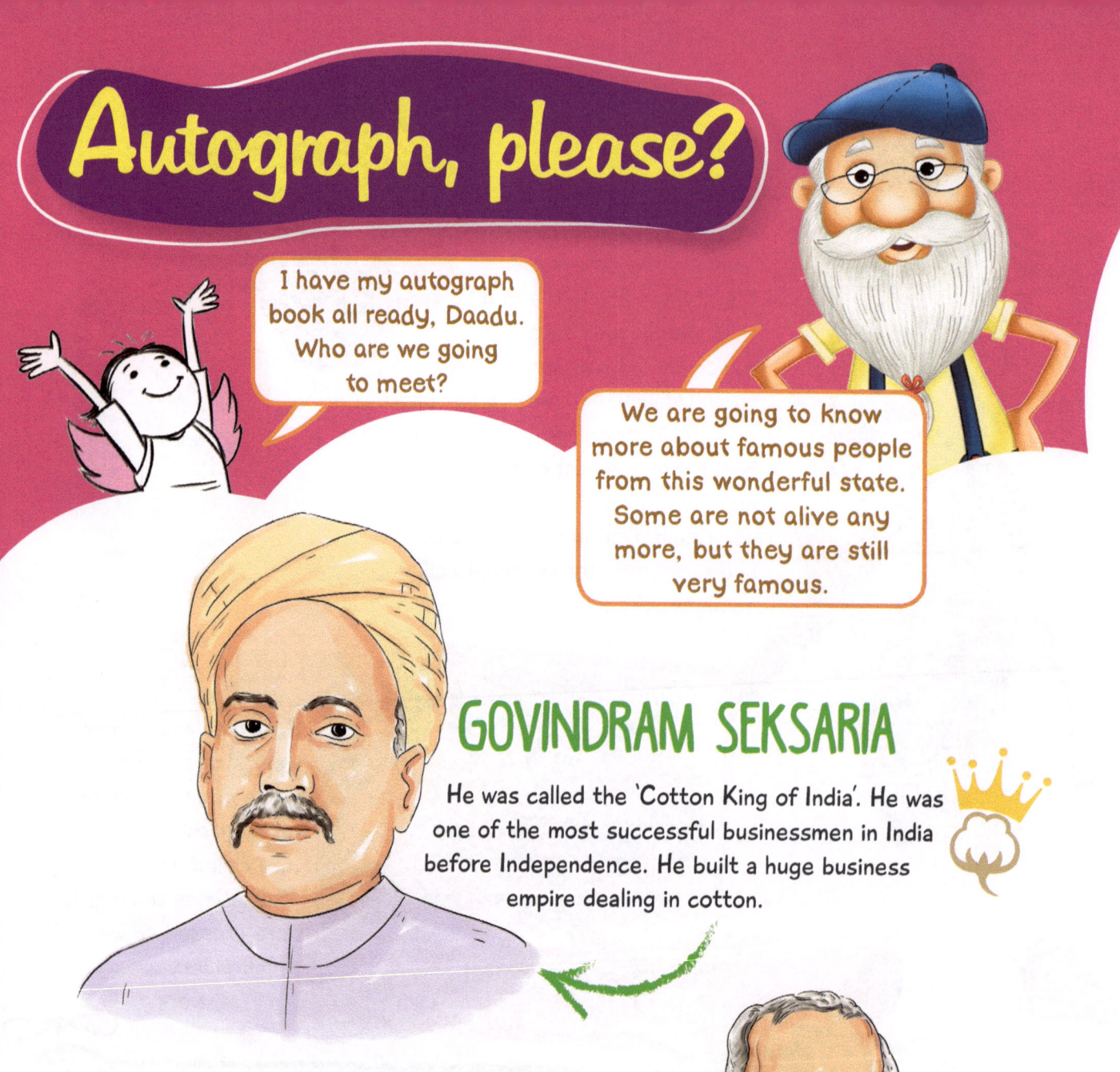

MAHARANI GAYATRI DEVI

Though born in another state, and with mixed parentage, Maharani Gayatri Devi was married into Rajasthani royalty. She was famous for her beauty and because she became a politician who worked for the people.

G.D. BIRLA

He was a famous businessman who started the Birla business empire, which today has offices all over the world.

MEERABAI

She was a Rajput queen known for her devotion to Lord Krishna. She wrote many songs in his praise that people still sing. These are called Meera bhajans.

Lord Krishna

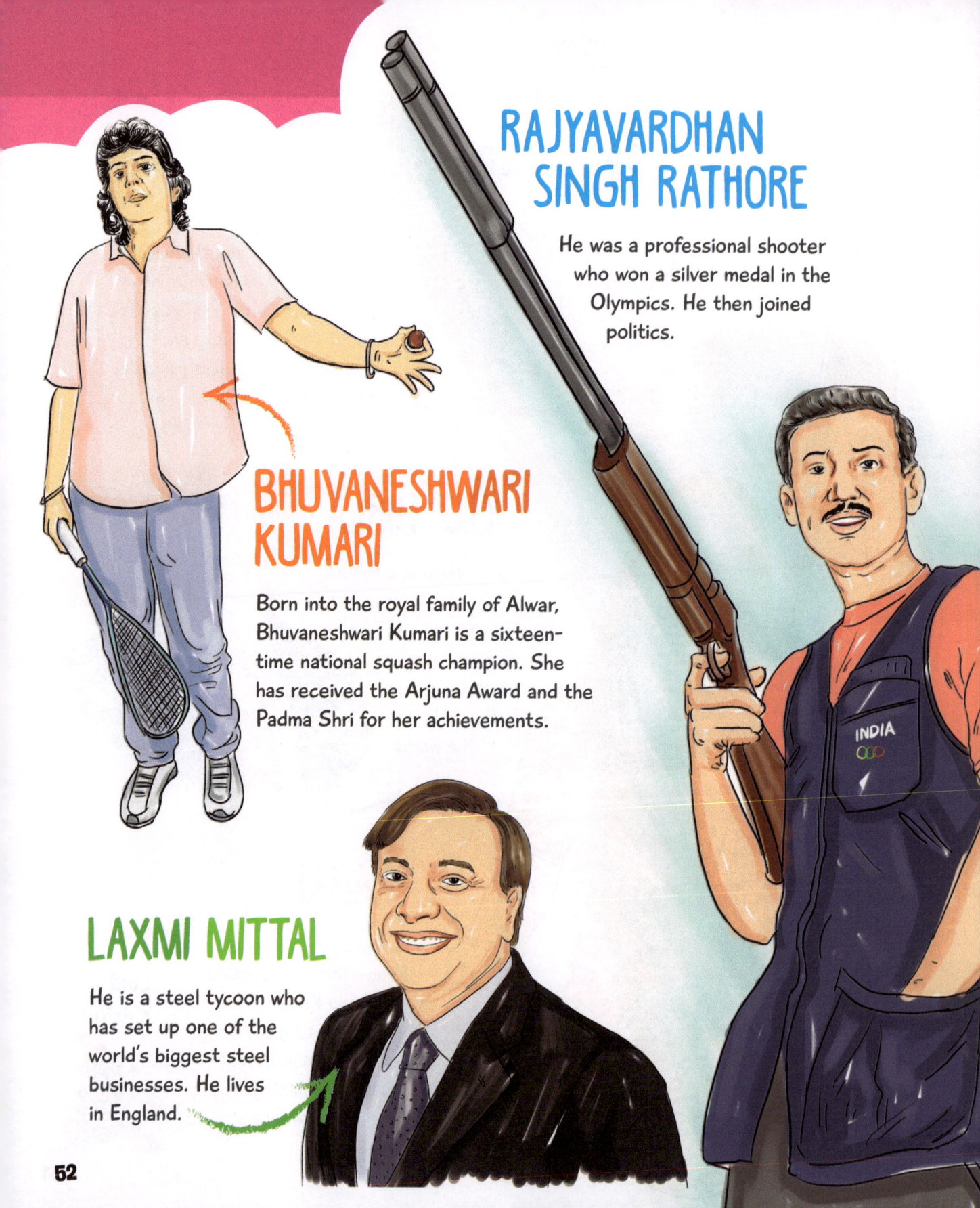

RAJYAVARDHAN SINGH RATHORE

He was a professional shooter who won a silver medal in the Olympics. He then joined politics.

BHUVANESHWARI KUMARI

Born into the royal family of Alwar, Bhuvaneshwari Kumari is a sixteen-time national squash champion. She has received the Arjuna Award and the Padma Shri for her achievements.

LAXMI MITTAL

He is a steel tycoon who has set up one of the world's biggest steel businesses. He lives in England.

ILA ARUN

She is a famous singer who is known for the way she brings Rajasthani folk songs to life. She has also acted in Hindi movies.

JAMNALAL BAJAJ

He was a businessmen who did a lot for people. He built an empire and also built schools and colleges so that children could get a better education.

GRID OF FAME

There are six famous Rajasthanis hidden in this grid? Can you find them all?

G	A	Y	A	T	R	I	T	A	B
I	L	A	A	R	U	N	S	C	A
S	F	E	R	H	A	N	D	T	J
M	E	E	R	A	B	A	I	W	A
B	V	B	I	R	L	A	E	E	J
M	I	T	T	A	L	F	D	G	J

Once upon a time . . .

Daadu, I'd love to hear a story from Rajasthan.

Rajasthan is full of stories and legends of days gone by. Listen to this story.

THE SEVEN SISTERS

At the edge of the vast Thar Desert lived a wealthy man called Aamod Singh. He lived with his seven daughters in a big haveli he had built by himself. There were no other houses around. But there were two demons called Shakasur and Bhikasur who roamed the desert at night, terrorizing travellers. Everyone lived in dread of them. And Aamod Singh was no different.

The haveli in which Aamod Singh lived had seven doors. To keep the haveli safe from the demons, Aamod Singh gave the job of locking the doors to each of his daughters.

'Every night, before you go to bed, one of you has to lock all seven doors,' he told them. 'This way each of you will have to do it just once a week.'

The seven sisters diligently did their job every night.

But one night, Lilavati, the youngest sister, was very tired. She locked door after door, but by the time she reached the seventh door, she was exhausted, for the haveli was very large indeed.

One door remained unlocked. She fell asleep right next to the unlocked door.

The silent desert night wore on as man and beast were fast asleep. But the demons were awake and prowling the desert. One of the demons, Shakasur, saw light pouring out of a door in Aamod Singh's haveli.

Aha! Here's my next victim, he thought to himself. He crept into the house through the open door. He saw Lilavati fast asleep, so he picked her up and put her into a sack.

'I shall take her home. She will cook and clean for me. She will be my prisoner,' he chuckled gleefully. On the way home, he felt tired. He put the sack down and decided to rest. Soon, he was fast asleep.

He woke up when the desert sun was high in the sky. He picked up the sack and trudged home. The sack seemed heavier than before.

When he reached home he opened the sack. To his anger, there was no Lilavati. Instead, the sack was full of rocks. Lilavati had cleverly filled the sack with stones and had run off home.

'Wait till I get my hands on her!' Shakasur thundered. He rushed to the Aamod haveli.

He reached the haveli and roared, 'Where is that girl?' To his surprise, he saw Lilavati's six sisters weeping. Instead of being afraid of him, they came rushing to him.

'Oh, Shakasur, that nasty demon Bhikasur has taken away our sister. He said he stole her from you and that you would be too afraid of him to get her back. Please go and get her back for us,' they wept.

'Grrrrrrrrrr,' Shakasur growled angrily. 'How dare that lily-livered Bhikasur talk about me like that. I will kill him.' Saying that, he stomped off to find Bhikasur.

As soon as he went, Lilavati popped out from behind a curtain, clapping her hands. This was all part of her cunning ploy.

Shakasur and Bhikasur got into a fierce fight. Using all the powers they had, they fought all day and all night. They each shot a magical arrow into the other and soon both were dead.

Lilavati's clever plan had saved her family and the entire village from the nasty demons Shakasur and Bhikasur.

TRAVEL DIARY

Have you enjoyed this trip to Rajasthan with your friends Mishki and Pushka—and, of course, with Daadu Dolma?

Now you can make your own Rajasthan diary. And if you ever visit Rajasthan, make sure you take pictures and put them in the photo box.

The first place I would visit in Rajasthan:

_____

If I ever meet Rana Sanga, this is what I would say to him:

_____

The one dish I am definitely going to eat:

_____

The monument I think is the most interesting:

_____

The one famous person from Rajasthan I would love to meet:

_____

If I were in Rajasthan, I would do this dance:

_____

The festival from Rajasthan that I think is the most fun:

_____

The five words that I think describe Rajasthan the best are:

_____

_____

_____

_____

_____

My Rajasthan memories:

ANSWERS

page 9 WHAT'S ODD
OCEAN, SKYSCRAPERS, LUNI

page 11 PORCUPINE TWINS
B and D are the same.

page 15 HIDDEN WORDS
Here are some of the words you can form: ant, apt, art, jar, jut, nap, nut, pan, pat, pun, put, ran, rap, rat, run, rut, tap, tar, ajar, aunt, pant, para, part, prat, rant, runt, tarp, tuna, turn, apart, Japan

page 17 WORD GRID

B	A	B	U	R	A	H	S	N	A	S
P	R	A	T	A	P	S	I	N	G	H
S	A	S	D	M	U	G	H	A	L	S
R	A	T	H	O	R	F	F	G	H	M
X	V	B	N	M	G	T	P	T	A	Y
A	K	B	A	R	Q	W	E	R	T	H
R	R	A	N	A	S	A	N	G	A	N
D	Q	S	B	H	A	T	T	I	S	N

page 19 SPOT THE DIFFERENCE

page 21 MATCH THE WORDS
What?—Kay?; How much money?—Kitto peso?; Go—Jawo; Goodbye—Khamma Gani; Yes—Hamme; What is your name?—Tharo naam kay hai?

page 23 RHYME TIME
bling, bring, cling, ding, fling, ping, ring, sing, sling, sting, string, swing, thing, ting, wing, wring, zing

page 25 CROSSWORD TIME

page 35 AMAZING MAZE

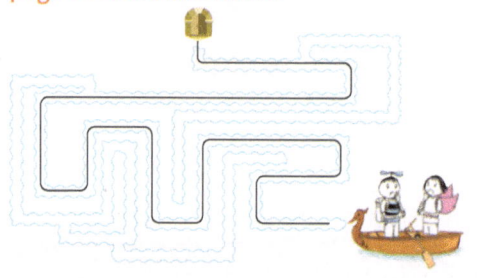

page 37 EXACTLY!!
B and C are the same.

page 39 WHAT'S ODD?
HAWA MAHAL, AKBAR, MUMBAI

page 41 PRECIOUS STONE SUDOKU

page 47 MIXED-UP WORDS
GUJIYA, GHEVAR, LAUNJI, BATI

page 49 TURBAN TRICK
B and D are the same.

page 53 GRID OF FAME

G	A	Y	A	T	R	I		T	A		B
I	L	A	A	R	U	N		S	C		A
S	F	E	R	H	A	N		D	T		J
M	E	E	R	A	B	A	I		W		A
B	V	B	I	R	L	A		E	E		J
M	I	T	T	A	L			F	D	G	J